A Man in Transition

A Man in Transition

✦

Reflections on Relationships, Leadership, and Life

Craig S. Galati

iUniverse, Inc.

New York Lincoln Shanghai

A Man in Transition
Reflections on Relationships, Leadership, and Life

iUniverse books may be ordered through booksellers or by contacting:

iUniverse
2021 Pine Lake Road, Suite 100
Lincoln, NE 68512
www.iuniverse.com
1-800-Authors (1-800-288-4677)

ISBN: 978-0-595-48176-7 (pbk)
ISBN: 978-0-595-60273-5 (ebk)

Printed in the United States of America

Contents

Introduction

One day I woke up and I wrote. I wrote from my heart. I wrote as if someone else was controlling my pen.

I told my wife about it. I had not written like this before. It must have been my creativity working overtime, trying to get out.

And I wrote ... I would sit at the table in my local Starbucks, not knowing what I was going to write about, and an hour later I had written things, things that were remarkable to me, things that I truly believe.

I shared my writing with some of my friends and family. They liked the direction I was going and they encouraged me to continue. I remember thinking, "I'm not sure where this is coming from or where it's going, but I'm going to ride it as long as I can."

There are many references to people, events, and places in the following essays. If you think you know them, you may. It can be our little secret.

If you like this collection, please tell everyone you know. If you don't, please forget that you read it.

I also have included a few lyrics from some of the songs that have inspired me over the years.

Writing has given new meaning to my life. It has opened up my mind, helped me to understand how I am feeling, and given me a vehicle to create a legacy of things in which I believe.

I hope you enjoy my journey.

Craig

Transitions

We are always in transition. Life is one big transition. We transition in and out of relationships, growing up, moving out, moving back in. We transition through school, get jobs, transition to careers, question everything, and transition to new jobs, new careers, and new relationships. We help our spouses, partners, and friends with their transitions. We teach our children how to transition from adolescence to adulthood.

For all the transitioning we do, is it any wonder why therapy, self-help books, reality TV shows and seminars are at an all time high in popularity?

What we need to do, but seldom do, is clearly understand what we want so we can make sense of the transitional nature of life. If we are clear with who we are and understand what we want, then we can embrace these transitions as learning opportunities.

Our species has questioned why we are here since the dawn of existence. I submit, we are here to transition, and that transition is a way of becoming closer to who we are so we can be one with the universe.

That is the final transition for all of us.

1

Relationships

There's a time and the time is now,
and it's right for me,
it's right for me,
and the time is now.

There's a word and the word is love,
and it's right for me,
it's right for me,
and the word is love.

YES
TIME AND A WORD

—Anderson/Foster
Copyright 1970 Cotillion, BMI

Do You Really Know Them

I picked up the paper. Found dead in his home, apparent suicide. I read it again, apparent suicide. How could this be? My hands trembled.

I knew him.

But did I really know him?

We were friends, not close friends, but friends just the same. I knew him for close to twenty years.

But did I really know him?

You think you know someone. I'm not sure we ever really do. It's unfortunate that one doesn't get close enough to really know what's going on inside another person.

What demons were tormenting him? What could be going on inside of him that was bad enough to consider taking his own life?

Maybe it was work …

Maybe it was home …

Maybe it was something else …

The point is, I didn't know him.

And now I never will.

Relationships

We all have relationships. Some are good, some are bad, some are in between. One of the things that defines us as human is our need for relationships. We love them, even though they don't always fulfill us, nurture us, or even love us back.

Sometimes we let go of relationships too soon. Sometimes we hang on to them too long. Sometimes they elude us even though we try as hard as we can to make them work.

There are all types of relationships; family, work, friends, and love. There are relationships we choose, and others that choose us. Some relationships only exist for two parties to accomplish something they could not do alone.

In my life, relationships have been very important. While I try to give to the relationship, unfortunately what I remember most is what I got from the relationship. But when I look back I wonder, did the other person get what he or she needed?

Although I know better, I very rarely seek enough feedback from the other party in the relationship. I talk about a lot of things: tasks and goals, but never talk enough about the essence of a relationship, the deep connections—the relationship itself.

Family relationships are the ones we are born into, the ones we never question, and the ones that have the greatest impact on our lives. They have a great effect on our ability to develop relationships but they are the ones on which we work the least. Do you know anyone who consciously worked on the relationship with his or her mother, father, sister or brother when they were young?

I'm not sure we have the capacity to nurture familial relationships when we are young. That puts tremendous burden on parents to learn how to develop and nurture relationships to model this positive behavior for their children.

If a child sees you paying attention to your relationships, perhaps he will remember that behavior and try to do the same when he becomes an adult.

Pay attention to the relationships in your life. It's not just for you and the other party; it's good for your children and their children too.

Commitment

Why are we so afraid to commit to something? Whether it is love, career, or our calling—most of us just kid ourselves that we are committed.

What does commitment look like? How does it feel?

I believe that true commitment is when you give yourself for the good of the person or thing to which you are committing and you do everything in your power to protect and nurture that person or thing.

Now, that doesn't mean that you don't get anything out of this commitment and it doesn't mean that you can only commit to one thing at a time. For instance, I believe that you can commit to love, family, and a career at the same time. It's not easy and it takes a cooperative effort between you, your lover, your family, and your coworkers, but it can be done.

Love is the commitment of two people to each other, but more importantly, the commitment to the relationship between the two. Commitment to love means paying attention to each other and doing things for the good of the relationship. When both people in love are committed to the relationship, problems and issues are much easier to resolve.

It's when one or both parties lose sight of the commitment they made to each other or forget about the mutuality required in a relationship that little problems grow to become big problems. When people quit paying attention to the relationship and ignore their commitment, they give up and let other things get in the way.

The same can be said about business. What is business, but a series of relationships and commitments? While these relationships may differ from love, business relationships are still about commitment.

The relationship between employer and employee, client and business, and between coworkers is commitment. It may feel more like a contractual arrangement at first, but I believe that when relationships work best, they grow well beyond contracts. Good relationships are based upon faith, trust, integrity and commitment.

I have been in my current business partnership for over twenty years. What I've learned in those twenty years is to be careful in understanding commitment. People can sometimes be committed to different things within the relationship yet not realize it. Clear communication is essential to develop understanding and mutuality within your relationships.

I believe that if you seek mutual commitment in your relationships, whether in love or in business, and if you work hard in preserving the integrity of the relationship, then you give yourself a chance for an engaged, fully transparent, and productive life.

Life is a Team Sport

Life is a team sport. There are many things we can do in life, but there are many things we can't.

Pick the best teammates to be a part of your life—those who have strengths where you have weaknesses and those who you want to help and for whom you care.

Pick teammates who care for you and will pick you up when you fall because one thing is certain: we all will fall.

Pick those teammates with whom you can develop relationships, real relationships that will be nurturing and engaging.

A good team needs a full complement of attitudes, capacities, capabilities and talents. Think of life as a team sport and surround yourself with those who can contribute to you and those to whom you wish to contribute.

Spend time together to develop your team synergy. To be a good team, you must practice.

Life can be incredibly difficult and incredibly fun at different times. Having the right team in place can help you get through the tough times and provide the friends to celebrate the good times.

What constitutes the right team? I heard a lecture by Dr. Will Miller several years ago where he brought forth a theory that we need our family relationships in our day to day lives to fully develop as human beings.

If your parents are not with you or live in another town, you need to augment this parental relationship. According to Miller, developing relationships with friends that augment the traditional brother and sister relationship is also essential.

I lost my father several years ago and this relationship has been difficult to replace. My mom tries to replace my relationship with my father, but she cannot, just as my father could never replace my relationship with my mother. I've had good success by associating with an older gentlemen who can offer fatherly advice. I think I can count on him and while this doesn't replace my relationship with my father, it certainly helps.

Another way to build your team is to surround yourself with those who can augment your skills. For instance, my skills lie in seeing the big picture and developing plans to get there. What I lack, however, is the patience to follow through with the plan. A perfect teammate for me is someone who loves follow-through and implementation. And I'm probably just the right teammate for them. Luckily, I've been able to find this relationship both in business and in my marriage.

Belonging to the right team will give you the opportunity to contribute to the well being of all of your teammates too.

The Power of Caring

We all want people to care about us. We want people to care about what we are doing, acknowledge our problems, issues, work, and the things at which we are successful.

It has been said that people won't care what you know until they know that you care. I truly believe this, and I've seen it in action over and over. Once you are able to demonstrate that you care for someone, there is a great opportunity to help him and develop a relationship. In fact, he will open up and be receptive to your offer of help.

I remember a contentious negotiation with a client. We were each at opposite ends of the spectrum and I was not sure we would be able to come to terms. The negotiation had become personal and neither party wanted to lose ground. I needed to try something different. I couldn't understand why the client didn't see how much I cared about his success.

I went home one night after a grueling session and reflected on the process. While the client probably realized that I cared about the project, I'm not sure that he knew that I cared about him. I decided to take a new tact. The next day when I walked into the meeting, I told the client that I would not leave until I knew that he was getting what he needed in this negotiation—that I cared about his position.

This floored the client, and after several hours of my questioning why his position was what it was, he began to soften. I learned that he had a new boss and it was important for him to look strong and in control to his boss. I suggested that we look at what we could do to make him look good to his boss and we spent the rest of the day considering various options that would achieve this goal.

As we talked, I noticed that he began to look out for me and understand my position—that I needed enough fee to really take care of him and make him look good in the long run. As I showed him my care, he began to care for me and we reached an equitable resolution.

Caring for people should come naturally to us, but somewhere along the path of life, we become more consumed with care for ourselves than care for others. Robert Greenleaf introduced us to servant leadership, but not many of us really practice it—or believe it.

The premise is that by serving you actually lead. I believe that by caring, you lead as well.

We're All On Our Own … Together

A wise man once told me that in life, we're all on our own together. I think what he meant was that even though it feels like we're alone when we face issues, we should feel comfort in knowing we're not the first, nor will we be the last to face the particular issue troubling us at the time.

Knowing others have overcome the very problem we are currently facing does help, but for me it seems to be more important to develop a support network of people who can help teach and mentor me along this journey. It is also equally important to me to be able to contribute to someone else, to teach them, and to share my experiences of life. It truly is a two-way street—a system of giving and taking—not always equal or in balance, but a karmic system none the less.

While we as a society cherish our independence and are taught that we need to solve our own problems, this shouldn't prevent us from seeking help or learning from others' experiences.

Every kid growing up thinks he knows better and that he doesn't need any help along life's journey. This may be true, but that shouldn't stop us as "elders" from offering our advice, counsel, and mentorship.

When I was young, I didn't seek advice from anyone. I thought that to ask someone for help was to be weak and vulnerable. How wrong I was.

I reinvented every solution on my own. If only I would have recognized that I was on the same path that every other member of the human race has been on at one time or another, and was confronting situations and issues that others had encountered thousands of times before me, I might have asked for help. Doing so could have saved me from myself, my fears, and my indecisions.

To recognize that we all need mentorship is not weakness; it is actually strength. It is what connects us as a species and it is how we keep our stories and history alive.

Besides, what will we do when we get old?

The Nurturing Kind

Relationships are like air. We need them to survive, but unlike air, we have to seek them out. They are plentiful, but you need to make an effort in order to see this abundance.

All of us have an innate need to connect to someone who will take the time to get to know us as we really are. While we don't readily admit it, we also need someone who will look behind our mask and is not afraid to help us expose our bones, our shortcomings, behaviors and insecurities.

Believe it or not, we all have an equally deep-rooted need to give that gift to someone else. We are born generous—it's later in life that we develop our baggage, put up our guards, and think only of ourselves.

Strong, long lasting, and deep relationships—the nurturing kind—are built upon this need to be generous.

Relationships start with what you can give, not with what you can get. When two people enter into a relationship with this in mind, a mutuality is developed that can take the relationship to great heights.

Remember that in any engagement, there are three parties: the two that want to be in the relationship, and the relationship itself.

I have been married for almost twenty-five years. In that time, I've learned that if it is important to you to stay in the relationship, you will. When times are tough and communication is difficult, focusing on the reasons you are in the relationship will help you overcome these difficulties.

Nurture the people with whom you want to be in relationship. Nurture and protect the relationship itself.

Your rewards will be greater than you can imagine.

The Power of Intention

Have you ever done something for the wrong reason? How did it work out? My guess is it wasn't as fulfilling as you had hoped.

In my life, there are many times when I have done good things but tainted them with selfish motives. I'm sure we all have done similar things like:

- Giving your boss a gift around review time to get a better raise;
- Not addressing a problem employee because that employee has good business connections;
- Pushing your employees or kids into something for your own selfish benefit.

When you do these things, things that are good in and of themselves, without pure intentions, it is kind of like wearing a shirt that says "I'm only here for me."

People see right through your actions to your real intentions. It's karma, and it is probably what has bred most of the cynicism in our society.

If you truly want to give your boss a gift, do so. But don't expect that the influence of a gift should change anything, except possibly her perception of you.

If you believe in the mission of a non-profit volunteer organization, then join it to help fulfill that mission. Meeting people and building relationships will be a natural by-product of the work. Remember that most people who sit on boards and committees do so because they believe in the organization. They can see when someone is motivated by reasons different from their own.

Don't push your employees or children into activities for your own personal gain. Show them the opportunities amd benefits and let them choose.

Intentions are powerful. They precede us in everything we do.

How many times have you done the wrong things for the right reasons? While they don't always work out, the recovery time is significantly shorter and you are able to maintain your integrity during the process.

I remember once being asked by a colleague of mine to attend a public hearing and testify on his behalf, based on my knowledge of him and his company's performance. At the same time, I was negotiating a contract with the same governing agency. Hindsight being what it is, I did not see the relationship between these two events at that time.

I went and testified on my colleague's behalf. The governing agency was trying to disqualify his company from contracting with them based on the company's past performance. The project the governing agency used as an example was one in which my firm was also involved. My colleague's company's performance was exemplary and I testified as such.

The very next day, the governing agency called me and broke off negotiations on my firm's contract. While I wished I would have thought about the situation more thoroughly, my intentions were good. I may have lost a contract, but I maintained my integrity and spoke up about what I believed to be true.

Over the years the staff has changed at that governing agency, and eventually we were awarded contracts with them. For me, the important thing is that I did not need to compromise my integrity to get these new contracts.

While intentions can't always ensure that you act accordingly, they certainly help in understanding whether or not you should do something in the first place.

Be clear in the reasons you want to do something and match your strategy to your intentions.

How many people do you know who appear to be in positions of authority for the purposes of feathering their own nests?

How many politicians appear to be in their positions for the power instead of to serve?

These people stick out like a sore thumb and everybody can see it!

Seek clarity in your life. Understand who you are and live within those intentions.

2

Leadership

You teach your children some fashion sense, and they'll fashion some of their own.

THE TRAGICALLY HIP
DON'T WAKE DADDY

—Copyright 1996 The Tragically Hip

Firing a Friend

I feel terrible. I need to fire a friend. I feel terrible.

I owe it to myself, my partners, my employees, my company—even though it's incredibly difficult. How did we get to this?

I guess friendships get in the way of doing the right thing. Deep in my heart, I know it is the right thing, but I also know the friendship will be lost.

My mind is filled with questions:

Did I try hard enough to correct the problem? Will this come as a surprise? Did I mask the problem? Would I feel this way if I wasn't dealing with a friend? Can or will this person change?

My mind is made up. I don't care about the questions. Right? I don't care or maybe I care too much. Is this care misdirected?

Will I have the courage to do it? How will I do it? When?

Soon. I need to act quickly before I lose another good employee who is tired of the inaction.

I need to fire a friend.

The company's watching.

Leadership

It takes a lot of courage to be a leader. Leaders are always subject to more criticism than are followers.

To be a leader, one needs to be an effective listener, to develop strong empathy skills, and learn to allow your intuition to come forward. A leader also needs to clearly understand that he does not have the answers—a leader cannot and should not try to solve the world's problems in a vacuum.

Effective leaders develop the best questions, which in turn help others develop the best solutions. The most effective leaders have an ability to inspire people and then get out of their way.

One of the fallacies of modern society is that we are taught that talking or advocating our opinion is leadership. While the ability to voice is part of it, too much emphasis is placed on a leader's voice. More emphasis should be placed on a leader's ability to listen to understand the issue or situation clearly enough to formulate questions that will lead to the best answers.

Great leadership is something that too often is talked about and rarely modeled in our organizations. The best way to teach leadership is to demonstrate it through daily behaviors.

Another misconception about leadership is that it is an identity.

Leadership is an activity.

The mere fact that someone owns a company or is placed in a position of authority does not make him a leader.

Leadership can be found at all levels and places within our organizations. The best leaders recognize this and create an environment where other, less authoritative leaders can flourish.

What have you done to foster leadership in your organization?

Leadership and Authority

In many companies in America, leadership is taken, not gifted. What I mean to say is that in many organizations, people assume leadership just because of status or authority—and others within those organizations let them.

Leadership through authority is not true leadership. Leadership through authority is coercion.

When people in authority take leadership, often they do not understand the basic tenets of leadership. They are the "take control, command, follow me up the hill" leaders and they misapply this leadership style to every situation. We, those of us who let them, become their co-conspirators.

I believe in servant leadership and leadership by example. I do not mean to diminish other styles of leadership such as, directive, supportive, and inspirational, which are all valid in their own right and serve certain situations well.

For instance, in a period of crisis, emergency, or public safety which requires quick response, a directive leadership style would be absolutely appropriate.

Inspirational leadership often works well when one is trying to encourage a group to rally around a cause or issue.

Even in these two examples, however, it is more important how a leader approaches the situation than what style she uses. As long as a leader is serving a greater need, people will see that, and it will lead to successful engagements with those within the organization.

Change vs. Resistance

I used to think I could force organizational change. I thought that by convincing people change was necessary and showing them what that change should be, it would just happen.

I was wrong.

I woefully underestimated the resistance to change, and I clearly did not understand what dynamics needed to be in place in my organization for change to occur.

I remember many staff meetings trying to get our employees to rally around a new vision—we were not going to be "just" architects any more. We wanted to completely change our practice and perform our services differently. When we presented this vision, we were either met with a "deer in the headlights" look or a unyielding mindset. As one staff member put it, "They can practice the way they want, but I'm going to pratice like an architect."

I learned that I can no more change an organization or a person than I can move a mountain or make someone love me. It's just not that simple.

What I can do, however, is change myself, and through my own personal changes, see the world in a different way. And perhaps, through this inner work, become the change I want to see in the world—a catalyst.

I spent many sleepless nights reflecting on myself, my habits, my behaviors, and my actions in an attempt to see how I was contributing to this resistance to change. What I found was that my actions were not in alignment with the change I wanted. Instead, I was infusing the organization with the stereotypical authoritative message of "do as I say, not as I do."

It takes deep personal commitment to be that change. People won't initially understand what you are going through or why. I truly believe that if the situation isn't working, although I may not be able to change the situation, I can certainly change how I view and interact with it.

For instance, I do not like what is happening to my chosen profession, architecture. The profession is not as valued as it was once was, either by clients or my colleagues within the profession.

I know I cannot change the profession. I cannot change the way clients view architects or the way architects view themselves. But I can choose to view myself in the way I want to be seen and I can align my actions with the way I want to interact with the world.

I have discovered there is incredible power in taking this viewpoint. Rather than complaining about the profession and its diminished value, I have changed myself.

I've become more value-focused and more confident. Instead of taking on work for work's sake, I focus on only taking work that is a good fit for our firm and even then, only where we can truly bring value. I began looking at my practice as a consultancy instead of as an architectural firm. Being a consultancy helps us look at the real needs of a client instead of trying to solve the client's stated needs through architectural work. Once we truly understand their needs, we can then assemble the appropriate professionals to help them.

The results are amazing. By focusing on my own inner change, people both within and outside of the profession view me in a different way. They see me and my firm in the ways I want them to see us.

This has done wonders for my firm. It has allowed us to differentiate in the marketplace and helped us find clients and employees who are aligned with our offering.

We don't need to "play the game" anymore. We can be who we are and find abundance in our potential.

So, why is this essay included in the leadership chapter?

If you want to lead change within your organization, start with yourself. That is true leadership.

Reflection-the Leader's Duty

Of all of a leader's responsibilities and duties, reflection is one of the most important. Reflection brings clarity to the other things a leader does.

What is reflection? Reflection is the time required to think, re-think, and contemplate situations, issues, and new thoughts. It provides our renewed energy and it gives us time to run potential ideas through our mind, to review various outcomes, identify possible solutions to problems.

Reflective time should not be used for playing the devil's advocate or for looking for the holes in the ideas. Rather, it should be used to let ideas blossom, emerge, and build upon each other. Staying positive in reflection allows us to be open to the possibilities that we might otherwise miss.

I often wonder how many good ideas or concepts I have talked myself out of before I learned to be positive in my reflection time. How many ideas were quashed before they were allowed to germinate and bloom? Reflective time should be used to let the mind soar, connect with the heart, and to let go of preconceptions.

If you look back on recent history, some crazy ideas stand out:

- Putting a man on the moon;
- Inventing and accepting the Internet;
- Believing that people line up and pay $5 for a cup of coffee because of the experience;
- Creating the iPod.

The devil's advocate could have easily killed those great ideas:

- We'll never have enough money to put a man on the moon and bring him home safely;
- Who would put away an encyclopedia and conduct research on a computer?
- $5 for a cup of coffee?
- People will not give up their 8-tracks, cassettes and CDs for something intangible—a music file?

Do you use reflection time in your business? Do you make time or do you think you are too busy? If you think you are too busy, just know that it is only the break-through ideas that you are keeping from yourself.

Find the time for reflection. Find a place. Find a way that works for you, any way, but find it, and let your mind wander and dream.

My favorite way to work reflection into my life is by walking early in the morning or going to my local Starbucks, paying my five dollars, plugging in my iPod and just thinking. I keep a journal of my thoughts, and the physical release of capturing my thoughts on paper inspires me to think of other related or non-related ideas. The process becomes a self-generating forum of thoughts and creativity.

Some people like to be outside, some like to stay up late in front of the fireplace, and some like to go for a drive. The point is—find what works best for you and reflect regularly. You'll be thankful that you worked reflection into your life.

Growing by Numbers

One of the problems I see with the current professional business model is the way it is structured to grow revenue by adding employees. This model relies on leveraging the low-dollar worker to perform minimally supervised tasks and may be one of the forces behind the commoditization of the professions.

This model leads a professional service firm to be constantly on the lookout for new employees, even when qualified, potential employees do not exist. It also starts the cycle of taking on work for work's sake, to feed the insatiable need to keep those new employees busy enough to grow revenue. This practice is, by its nature, difficult to sustain.

One fact not many professionals working within this business model realize is that growth in revenue does not always result in higher profits.

I've observed that this business model focuses a tremendous amount of energy on staying busy. That same energy could be used for other more important things including those that bring meaning to life—the things that fill life's passion.

But, instead, we're too busy feeding the fire.

What if we, as leaders of our respective organizations, flipped this business model on its ear and tried something different?

What if we focused our energies on building the capacity of our people?

What if we tried to grow our revenue by growing our people so that they could deliver higher value, rather than just higher numbers of chargeable hours?

The choice is ours. Did we become leaders in our companies to follow the antiquated business model of our predecessors, or did we become leaders because we wanted to lead change?

Did we strive to be leaders so we could work more and be busier, or did we dream of a better way of conducting business?

I have to believe we all dreamed of something better than the status quo business model. Why become a leader otherwise?

Not Acting … Is Acting

Talk is cheap. We've all heard that one before. In many organizations, there is the espoused culture, or the culture the organization wants the world to see, and the actual culture of the organization. Rarely do the two meet.

Everyone knows how we want our organizations to thrive. We have dreams, hopes, and desires for our organizations.

We also know how our organizations really exist, but sometimes we tell ourselves lies—including that our organizations are aligned with our dreams, hopes, and desires.

When we tell ourselves lies, we are actually undermining our organizations' ability to reach our desired dreams.

Our organizations need us to dream. They also need us to act. Our organizations need us to dream of the future and put plans in place to move the organization to the desired goals.

Our organizations need us to dream. They also need us to act to confront the reality of the organizations' true culture and close the gaps between this reality and the organizations' desired culture.

Not dreaming is not dreaming, but not acting *is acting*.

The Unsolicited Offer

Every day we receive unsolicited offers from people selling services and products. Do you pay attention to them?

The essence of a successful unsolicited offer is offering something of value to someone who also sees it to be of value.

An unsolicited offer shouldn't need to be sold, just offered.

So how does this happen? First of all, I do not believe the shotgun approach works. Trying to sell something you think is valuable to the masses is difficult—or it takes a ton of money to accomplish.

I've found that to make an unsolicited offer work, you must be good at two things.

- Clarity—understanding what you have to offer, to whom it would be valuable, and why it would be valuable;
- Timing—the ability to sense within the marketplace when what you have becomes valuable to someone else.

The first one is relatively easy. You can determine what you have to offer, and through research you can develop a sense of who may value your offer. You just need to be careful that your passion for the offer doesn't taint your objectivity.

Getting the timing right takes patience, thought and practice. It also requires that you get out from behind your desk and meet people and it requires that you keep up with current trends and issues within your marketplace.

If you can get good at these two points, then the unsolicited offer, targeted successfully, can open doors for you that you only previously imagined.

Negotiation

I hate negotiating. At least I hate the type of negotiating that most people do. You know, win-lose, take it or leave it. The posturing, the games—they disgust me.

I approach things looking for win-win. When you approach things this way, you know you'll get what you need. My approach is to make sure the other party also gets what it needs.

This approach breaks down quickly, however, when the other party isn't looking out for you as well. When someone approaches the situation as win-lose, he won't be satisfied until he wins and you lose.

People in this situation are so distrusting. They view you from their mindset—"if they are trying to take advantage of you, you must be trying to take advantage of them."

So how do we break this cycle?

Refuse to negotiate this way. Don't give in to win-lose. Let the other person know that you are here to make sure that he is going to win in this negotiation, too. Be clear so that he knows that you will not settle for win-lose at yours or his expense. Ask a lot of questions—clarify when the other party wants something or doesn't agree with something. It is through this inquiry that you can begin to appreciate his position and truly be able to seek a win-win resolution.

Negotiations are very important—many times they are the beginning of a relationship. Be careful to start a new relationship off on the right foot. A relationship built upon trust and the ability to seek mutuality has a good chance of being fruitful.

Passing the Torch

Who will be the future leaders of your organization? Do you have the next generation in place, or do you hope the right person will walk into your organization just in time for you to depart?

We have all heard the horror stories of organizations that dissolved when the leaders of that business retired or died.

I know of a very successful professional service firm that went bankrupt within two years of its founder's retirement. That firm's fate was not a result of a lack of talent within the organization, but rather a result of the gap in leadership that occurred upon the founder's retirement. The founder's neglect of the essential succession planning functions of mentoring and coaching cost the firm its life.

Far too many leaders, whether doctors, lawyers, coaches, or accountants don't think of leadership and ownership transition until they begin contemplating their own retirement.

By then, it's too late.

Ownership transition is relatively easy—it's simply a transaction. Leadership transition is far more difficult because it is a process. It takes several years, and involves more than just an agreement. It involves:

- A leader that is willing to coach and teach;
- A future leader that is willing to learn and think differently about his or her role;
- A leader that can let go;

- A future leader that will step up to the plate;

- A staff that will accept a change in leadership; and

- A marketplace that accepts the new leadership of the organization.

When you look around your organization to determine if you have the future leaders in place, be honest with yourself. The most competent workers with the best technical skills do not always become the best leaders.

Our tendency is to promote from within, but that is not always the best choice. Don't force it if it isn't in the best interest of the organization.

Look critically at the people you have and ask yourself, "Does this person have the ability and capacity to lead? Would I follow him?"

If the answers are 'yes,' then you are one of the lucky few. It is now time to start some of the most rewarding work you will ever do—teaching and passing your wisdom on to the next generation.

Here are some thoughts to guide you:

- Dedicate your time, energy, and money to make a successful transition happen;

- Plan the transition carefully, and include the future leaders in the planning;

- Be clear about your intentions with the future leaders as well as with others in your organization;

- Create a safety net for the future leaders on which they can count—but don't let them use it as a crutch;

- Let go of the small decisions to allow the future leaders to build confidence in themselves; and

- Don't undo those decisions unless you absolutely must. Sometimes we need to learn from our mistakes.

Others Before Self

Many people have written and spoken about the need for serving other's needs before our own. While conceptually I buy into this concept, I'm not really sure I've practiced it to the fullest. Certainly I have tried to serve others, but in doing so, I have also tried to make the process a win-win, to get something for myself in the deal.

I know many people who are just the opposite. You probably do, too. They are the ones who serve their interests first, and if other's needs get satisfied at the same time, fine. These are the people we speak about in hushed tones.

"If we can make him think it is his idea, we'll be able to do it!"

"We need to make it fit his agenda; then maybe we can work for the common good."

As I said, I've tried to reach those win-wins, to get what I need while serving the other's needs.

So what do I do now? I have been asked by my organization to put my needs aside, on hold, to fully commit to the needs of the organization.

I've been asked to put my aspirations, goals, and personal agenda aside for the good of the organization.

What does it mean to truly serve other's needs before self?

I will soon find out.

Make Room for New Ideas

In business, everyone thinks they know what to do—or do they just act like they do? I will admit that I don't know what to do in every situation. Even in the situations in which I think I do know exactly what to do, there is always another solution—and maybe even a better way.

What I've found, however, is that people want to hold onto their ideas too long. They don't listen to a new idea long enough to determine its merit before they move to action. This need to act at times polarizes their potential, and it certainly diminishes the potential of the situation.

I remember years ago working for a gentleman who was very egocentric and controlling. He never let my ideas be included in any discussion. His demeanor was the same with clients as well. Over the years, many talented professionals left his office and built very successful practices of their own. Practices which competed with their former employer's practice.

It is not easy, but each one of us should learn to suspend our ideas and allow ourselves to become open to the influx of new ideas. I cannot guarantee success if you do this, but I will guarantee that you will make better decisions and have more fruitful engagements with others as a direct result of employing the practice of suspending judgement and considering others' ideas.

Remember, everyone has good ideas. We all want to be heard and we all love engaging in stimulating conversations.

Each of us holds the key to being heard when we speak—and the key is in making room for new ideas.

3

Life

You're hanging around the day,
You're fooling yourself with blame,
You're taking it all to future site,
Hanging around today,
God only knows what you're missing.

THE POLYPHONIC SPREE
HANGING AROUND THE DAY, PART 2

A Moment of Silence

I attended a local housing board meeting the other day.

During the meeting the Chairman asked for a moment of silence for those who had died in the development over the last month.

A moment of silence.

Is that the reason we live our lives?

Every waking hour, every breath takes us closer to a moment of silence? I suggest we live our lives to the fullest—that we enjoy every moment—silent or not.

With a moment of silence to look forward to as our reward, the journey becomes even *more* important.

The Art of Growing Up

As I watch my children grow up, I am struck by the ease with which they handle challenges in their lives. Things I think would bother them, don't faze them, and things I think would not bother them, bother them terribly.

I guess it's a matter of perspective. We tend to view others' issues in terms of how we see them. While we are growing up, we are taught, we learn, and we experience many things that shape our perspective. And this perspective, in turn, shapes us, becomes core to our understanding of life's situations, shapes our relationships with others, and even contributes to how we shape others.

So what does this mean? Are we a product of our environment? Have we given up, or did we ever have free will?

Thinking that even a portion of our lives might be predetermined is a disturbing thought to me. If our sensibilities of situations are developed so early in our life and become determinants to our life, than why do we value free choice so highly in our society?

It is my belief that some aspects of who you are and what you are meant to be are hard-wired into each of us. These aspects were put there during our creation and molded over the years by our parents, teachers, friends, and employers.

But many aspects of us are not hard-wired. They are learned, and they are within our control. The problem is many of these items cannot be linked through traditional cause and effect models. We all think we can determine effect by our actions but the world is far too complex for this.

For instance, if we greet our coworker with a smile and a friendly hello, the logical effect will be a return smile and hello. But, is there something bigger that could happen from this gesture that is not as closely linked?

Could this simple gesture be passed along to others? Perhaps. Could it help someone get through a particularly tough time in his life? Perhaps.

We don't know for sure. But we do know that most human beings need and want to be greeted with that friendly smile and hello.

In looking back to times with my children, I see many times when I let my personal issues get in the way of greeting them with that smile.

What am I teaching them?

- My issues are more important than them;
- They shouldn't care about others;
- They should become obsessed with how they feel.

I hope not.

While we can't change the pre-determined aspects of ourselves, our children, and our coworkers, we can have a profound impact on the things they learn.

Teach by example.

Differences and Similarities

What's wrong with kids these days?

As I sit in my local Starbucks, I look at a group of three late teens, two boys and one girl, engaged in deep conversation.

The girl has two-tone hair, clearly neither color her own. The boys both wear baseball hats cocked sideways in a manner I would never do. All three have more piercings than I can count, pants worn low, large studs on their belts.

As they sit and talk, I am struck by their ability to multi-task—text messaging, talking on the telephone, reading and conversing at the same time.

But what really strikes me is the quality and normalcy of their conversation—not too dissimilar to the types of conversation that I had with my friends some thirty years ago.

Problems at school;

Problems with parents;

Girlfriends, boyfriends;

Homework;

"What are we doing on Saturday?"

While we may look different, I find great delight in our similarities. This new generation is going through the same things we did, but at a time of greater speed and change in the world.

The younger generation needs to deal with things we never dreamed of—AIDS, global warming, information overload, eroding societal values, and depleted natural resources just to name a few.

We saw the fall of Communism, a man walking on the moon, and civil unrest that tore our nation apart. They've already seen a terrorist attack on American soil, sexual transgression in the White House, a President elected without the popular vote, and a world that is shrinking every day.

The speed of information transfer with the Internet, YouTube, and MySpace is incredible. Mistakes that one makes when that person is growing up can reach millions of people seconds after they are made. A posting made on line remains to haunt the young person throughout their life.

How are these kids able to cope? Are we leaving their world better or worse? What will they see? What does the future hold for them?

I'm startled out of my pondering.

"Do you think she'll ask me to the Sadie Hawkins dance?"

Giving Back

Great communities aren't born, they are built. If you look at any great community, you will find several individuals who have given of their time and money to make that community great. That is no coincidence. Communities are about people, and people invest their time and resources into the things they love.

There are many things our communities need that government and private enterprise cannot provide. It is a good thing that many individuals recognize this void and are willing to fill it.

Whether by sitting on a Board, helping deliver meals to the elderly, or coaching children in a sport, pick something you love and give of your time. Find others who can give of their time and money, too, and invite them in. The experience you will have is worth it.

The things we can accomplish together are incredible and very much needed within our community. You'll get a lot out of giving of your time. You'll meet like-minded people, build worthwhile relationships and networks, and you'll help those who really need it.

I've been fortunate to hold several leadership positions in non-profit corporations, as well as having held a seat on the Las Vegas Planning Commission from 1997-2003, including chairing the Commission in 2001 and 2002.

I learned a tremendous amount about leadership, politics, and human dynamics during those tenures. These lessons have been invaluable to my career and I was able to learn them while making significant contributions to my community.

We all want to be able to contribute—it is a deep, inner need. We all have a need to be a part of something bigger than ourselves, to belong. We want to feel good about ourselves and we want to be a part of good things.

So, what are you waiting for? Give back and you shall receive.

We all seem to do this around holiday time. What I'm suggesting is that you should work this giving into your life year-round. It will contribute to a rich and fulfilled life.

Midsummer of Life

Never to see spring again! A startling thought indeed.

I've reached the midsummer of my life. As I look back, I wonder if I did the right things—work, career, love, life. I am happy, so I guess the answer is "yes."

My springtime was filled with all the good things of spring—new birth, new life, a renewed energy. I can still smell the flowers, the fragrant bouquet of spring in the desert. I can still see the new leaves forcing themselves from the branches and stems—their newness, their fragility, their vibrancy—coming to life without knowing that the harsh summer is coming. The innocence of it all is overwhelming.

Midsummer is a good time. It is baseball season and there still is a chance of winning the pennant. Hope is eternal.

It is hard to believe that I am at the midsummer of life. I still have a beginner's mind in many ways. But, in other ways, I am very different. I am much wiser about who I am and what my destiny may hold.

I love the quality of the light in midsummer. Although at times it is harsh and reflective, there is something very refreshing knowing that the sun is still burning this brightly. The morning sun peeks over the mountains creating colors only God could have imagined—orange, pink, red—mixed together, they take your breath away. I never appreciated these colors in spring, although I am sure now they were always there.

Midsummer also means vacation, a time to do what you want—what you were meant to do. Spring cleaning is over and it is time to relax and let your mind wander. I've heard summer called the "dog days". But that is not how I feel. Midsummer is a time for reflection and a time of new purpose. I finally have the capacity to make good decisions. Not the quick, knee-jerk, clumsy decisions I made in spring. I now know that things will turn out pretty much the way I choose.

I thought that midsummer would be a sad time, knowing that I will never see spring again. I was wrong. I now have the ability to appreciate summer and I owe it to the things I learned in the spring. Spring was about trying things, making mistakes—miscalculating the rain, miscalculating the wind.

Midsummer is still about trying things, but more purposefully. Oh … and midsummer is about writing. Putting pen to paper and letting thoughts flow. Sharing, teaching and wanting to let people know that midsummer is a wonderful time.

There is still a lot of summer left. I intend to enjoy every single minute of it, every drop of sun, every breeze, every summer storm, and every glass of lemonade.

I will embrace midsummer—for fall is coming!

A Time for Thanks

As Americans hustle and bustle about—traveling, cooking and gathering family and friends, I ponder the origin of Thanksgiving.

As we learned in school, the Pilgrims were grateful for what the new world provided them. And they were astounded with the help they received adapting to a new way from a different people. The Pilgrims, being smart and concerned for their survival, opted to invite their neighbors over to thank them and ensure peace.

But what has happened since those days? As Americans, why didn't we take the Pilgrims' cue to heart? Why have we let Thanksgiving deteriorate to "just another Holiday?"

I submit that Thanksgiving should not be just about connecting family and friends, but could be a great opportunity to fuel the bonds of people of all ages, races, genders and social status. The opportunity to share a feast with people you don't know could start something special—something that America really needs—connections and community.

While this simple gesture could be good for America, why stop there? Couldn't we give thanks to our neighbors, family, friends, coworkers and people we meet each and every day?

What if we really could develop true appreciation for the things we have instead of just wishing for more? Let's try to appreciate the simple acts of our friends and coworkers as a start. Let's start cherishing the time we have together, the fun we have together, and the opportunity to really give thanks.

The Pilgrims came to this country to escape persecution. They came to start a new life. That should inspire us to think differently next Thanksgiving.

The Tipping Point

In most of my twenty plus years in my career as an architect and consultant, it has felt like pushing a boulder up a hill. Sure, those around me have helped push, but I've never felt I could take my hands off the boulder—not even for a second.

My colleagues and I have challenged the status quo, sacrificed our earning potential, and given of ourselves to do something different. We chose to offer care and empathy to our clients—not just services.

When it works, it really works, but there still is a disconnect between the offer and the delivery. Naively, I made the assumption that others with whom I work care the same way I do, or have the capacity to learn, develop empathy, and deliver on the promise with the same vigor as it was made.

What is it I am to do? Stop making the promise? Relax my standards? Move to another place? Start another firm?

The questions won't leave my head. I can't sleep. I can't think. I can't focus.

What is it I am to do?

I hold the boulder at the summit. It's been here for a year but it won't tip either way.

What is it I am to do?

My arms and legs strain to push the boulder over the top. My energy is depleted. Will I ever see the boulder move past the tipping point?

My friends and colleagues stand below. At times they push, but only for a brief period. Some stay longer, but they too become disenchanted and move to a different mountain.

I can't budge it—but it's not falling back.

The boulder must move. I have no more strength, but I cannot leave it here.

Fall to the promised land or fall back and crush me …

Either would be better than to be stuck at the tipping point.

Patience

Some say patience is a virtue. For me, it's just hard. But, it is something that needs to be exercised every day. Yes, just like a muscle, one needs to get one's patience into shape.

Why is having patience so important? Without patience, we may miss an opportunity. We might not wait long enough for a situation or idea to develop fully. But to have patience is not enough. Just as stretching and strength exercises need to be augmented with aerobics, patience needs to be paired with persistence.

Stretch, relax, stretch, relax, stretch—the combination of patience and persistence give you the best of both worlds.

Persistence gives us the ability to get things done and patience gives us the ability to do the right thing.

Nerves

Of all of the man-made constructs, the concept of being nervous is by far the one I understand the least. How come I still get nervous or anxious? Heck, I've been doing this for over twenty years. I've been successful. I've seen many situations, both good and bad. I've had great triumphs. I've lost jobs and I've lost loved ones. I've been sued, vindicated, and I've also lost lawsuits even when I was right.

So, I ask myself, why the nervousness and anxiety over certain situations? Perhaps it's because I care about what I'm doing. Perhaps it's because I build up things in my mind bigger than the situation. Perhaps I'm just hard-wired this way.

I am confident. The evidence would support the facts that if I put my mind to something, give it my best and use my skills and gifts, it will generally work out more times than not. So, why the nerves?

I overanalyze things. Maybe I should just go with the flow. God, I wish I could, but it's not in my nature. Do I have a fear of failure? I guess the answer is a timid "yes." But why? Look at the facts.

I think I'll try to chill. I know I'll do well, and if I don't—so what—I've faced greater adversity before.

OK, that's what I'll do. Chill.

I've convinced myself. I'm ready. I'm relaxed. I'm calm.

Time to go on-stage …

Here come those nerves again.

Positively Positive

Have you ever met that eternally positive person? The one that "never has a bad day?"

I did, and I wished I was more like them, so I began to practice. As I practiced seeing the world through a positive filter, my days did start getting better. People started engaging me in conversation more often and my relationships at home and work became more fulfilling and less argumentative.

I didn't change a single external thing!

I was still tired in the morning. I still got stuck in traffic. I still got hit with adversity, got caught in bureaucracy, and had to do things I didn't want to do. Even so, I felt better about all that was going on in my life.

The real change that needed to be made in my life was ME. I focused on the positive things going on around me (and there were plenty from which to choose.) When I focused on the positives, the problems didn't seem so big or insurmountable. The little things I didn't like about others went away and instead, opportunities presented themselves to me.

It is pretty cool how refocusing works. It is as simple as this; if you look for the good things in your life, you'll find them. If you focus on what's wrong with your life, you'll find that too.

This little experiment worked for me. Now my challenge is to keep it up and not slide into my old way of viewing the world!

The Past

I've heard people talk about needing to escape the past, to put the past behind them, to move on beyond the past.

While I don't disagree with the perspective of "not wanting to get stuck in the past," I would also submit that who you are today is a product of your past experiences. You are who you are because of the past, and who you will be tomorrow is because of what you are experiencing today.

So why not embrace the past as you move forward? Be cognizant of where you came from as you head to a new place. The lessons you learn today in the here and now will shape who you will become tomorrow.

Keep the artifacts from your past. Keep your writing, letters, and the work you produced. It will help remind you of how you became you.

It's All In The Gray

Great ideas have never been found with a black and white mindset. The best ideas and breakthroughs exist within the shades of gray. Black and white is an either-or mentality. Gray is a both-and mentality.

Most people are more comfortable in a black and white world. It's much harder living in the gray. Gray requires you to think, and the possibilities are endless. In the ambiguousness of gray, there is not a path—there is not a right or wrong way, but many right and many wrong ways.

It's more difficult to chart your course in gray, not because of the ambiguity, but because there are so many right paths. The key is finding the path that is most right for you.

If you are clear with what you want and why you want it, it will help you evaluate all of the possibilities that are available to you. It will help you sort through the endless opportunities to determine the one great idea that best suits you.

Get into the gray!

Fifteen Minutes of Fame

You've all heard the clichés:

"We all get fifteen minutes of fame," "The spotlight shines on every one of us eventually." It's a once in a lifetime opportunity."

If this is true, it raises a few thoughts for me:

- Why would the spotlight need to shine on me?
- If the spotlight does reach me, I had better be ready when it does;
- I had better not waste those fifteen minutes;
- If it really is a once in a lifetime opportunity, why is this the second time it has been presented to me?

I really don't subscribe to these clichés. If we only get fifteen minutes of fame, who cares? What does fame give us, anyway? How does it help us or others? Does it really matter?

Opportunities are presented to us every day, every hour, every minute. However, we only see very few of them and that's OK. Hopefully we see the ones that matter.

I once considered running for an elected office. My friends, my colleagues, supporters and special interest groups all told me, "it's a once in a lifetime opportunity." Maybe that was true, but I wasn't my opportunity. Besides, it was the third time the opportunity was presented to me. I will know when the time is right for me and I fully believe that it will be presented again.

I know many people who have had wonderful, caring, full and giving lives without any fame. It doesn't bother them, and in fact, they say that fame would get in the way of doing the work they were meant to do.

How grounded it would be to live this way—especially in our over-hyped, over-famed, over-saturated world.

I know we all love recognition. We love for people to know what we've done and why.

But it doesn't really matter. Not in the big scheme of things, and not in itself.

I'm Going Through Changes

Sometimes I don't recognize myself in the mirror. I'm sure it's me, but it's not how I remember myself. Gray used to be the color of clothes I wore.

I'm going through changes.

Other times when I look at myself, I see a new and improved version of me—still with the glimmer of youth in my eyes.

I'm going through changes.

I'm changing on the inside, too. Things that used to matter to me, don't matter anymore. I could care less of what people think of my looks and my physical abilities. I know if they take the time to get to know me, while they may not like me, they certainly will respect who I am—who I am becoming.

I'm going through changes.

I don't have time for the constant chatter, noise, and bantering about things that the media thinks I should care about. Who cares what Paris Hilton wore today? Who cares about all of the political posturing, saving face, covering tracks, back-room deals, and lies?

I'm going through changes.

I care about things with meaning to me. Things that touch the heart. Work that the helps people and makes a difference. Music. Time with family, education, organizations with purpose and conviction, books, art, things and places that are well designed. Clever things.

I'm going through changes.

Do you recognize me? I was always here. I'm not that different from you. I'm just not afraid to say it.

We're all going through changes.

Talking Without Words

The glow of happiness, the raised eyebrow, the smirk, shrug and nod.

We talk without words.

Glazed-over eyes, the smile, the shake, frown and stare.

We talk without words.

Sometimes I can tell what you're going to say before you say it. I can finish your sentence.

Other times, I cannot hear what you are saying, even when you carefully articulate it.

Being present and attentive seems to be the key to receiving the whole message.

Communication is much more than what is written or said. Our true emotions come out if we pay attention.

We talk without words.

Authenticity

How much time is wasted by not dealing with the issues, the feelings, and the things that get in the way?

There is so much time wasted that we've even invented a language for it.

- Beating around the bush;
- Stonewalling;
- Sugar-coating it;
- Being politically correct;
- Speaking in half truths.

Why don't we address things honestly and directly? I believe that answer is multi-faceted and is based more in how we internally receive messages than how we deliver the message. At least this is true for me.

I have a tendency to take things personally instead of just taking them in. I think there are many people like me who also do this.

Knowing and admitting that you take things personally could be the first step for change. Being cognizant of your tendencies and first reactions can help you remove them or at least suspend them.

So what does this have to do with authenticity?

We view our actions through our feelings—how we will react to something—and we shadow our beliefs onto other people.

When we have something to say to someone, we internally filter what we are going to say and how we think they will receive it, and the filter we use is "how would I receive it?" So, how we deliver our message and our ability to be authentic is grounded in our ability to receive the message and how personally we take things.

We worry that we will offend someone because we might be offended.

We worry that someone will take something wrong because we would take the same thing wrong.

We worry that someone will not have the ability to deal with something because we would not be able to deal with the same thing.

And we put the road blocks up.

We really don't know how someone is going to react to something and we really don't know if someone is going to be offended. We can't control that.

But we can control how we deliver the message and we can control the intention of why we're delivering the message.

Don't discount the power of intention.

One of the common qualities of high performing teams is their ability to deal with issues directly, authentically and quickly. They don't let things fester and get in the way of achieving that for which they are striving.

I believe that authenticity is the key to successful relationships.

I've found in my life that the issue is seldom the problem, but how I have dealt with the issue always impacts it.

Did I avoid the issue, or did I deal with it head on, directly, honestly, authentically and with pure intentions?

It is our choice.

Writing From a Dark Place

I have high hopes. I believe things will work out for the best, but it seems they never turn out the way I had planned.

Why am I in such a dark place?

There are days that I wake up with excitement—ready for the day and its possibilities. Then the problems mount—they grow out of proportion to their significance.

Why am I in such a dark place?

I live for energy. I am an externally focused person, and by that I mean that I get my energy from the world. I seek positive relationships. I seek potential in others.

Why am I in such a dark place?

I look back on my life and I notice that fall has always been tough for me. Maybe it's the time change—less sun in the evening. Maybe it's because fall reminds me of my father's death. Perhaps it is because fall has become some sort of a time of judgment, when all of the year's goals are measured. Maybe it's chemical—some sort of cosmic joke.

Perhaps it is a karmic solution to slow me down—to make me reflect and re-assess what is important. Just like the cycles of the day, perhaps I am to be on a yearly cycle and this time is to be used to rejuvenate, to rest, and to gain energy for the next push.

I should try to accept this time of darkness as the key to the future for me. I should view this time of the year as a positive—a necessary time of solace that is needed for me to be who I am.

Perhaps, if I start using this time positively, it won't feel like such a dark place.

Youthful Exuberance

No fear! It's not just a popular brand, it's a way of life for our youth. As I watch my kids, I see a bit of my youth. I wasn't afraid of anything. I knew I could accomplish anything. Fear never entered the equation. Kids don't overanalyze things. They just are who they are.

And then one day I grew up.

I don't remember the date exactly or the place or event, but one day a new emotion entered me, one that I'd not experienced before. I felt fear. I felt that maybe I wasn't going to accomplish something—maybe I needed to think it through, analyze it, rationalize it, or perhaps accept defeat.

And analyze it I did. I began to analyze everything. I tried to think things through to their logical conclusion. I began to think about the possibilities of not achieving—of failing. I became consumed with mapping out the right plan for success. I became afraid of failing. Perhaps I will not be successful and perhaps I will fail.

And the failures came. The more I acted out of the fear of failing, the more I failed. The more I worried, the more I needed to worry. How could this be happening?

It took me three very long and difficult years to realize that I was the cause of these failures. By letting myself become consumed with fear, I'd lost my edge—lost my focus. It took another year to regain my confidence, but I did.

I remember the first time my business was sued. At the time, this was monumental and its fact consumed every waking moment of my life. Looking back fifteen years later, however, I know that lawsuits are a part of business and being sued doesn't necessarily mean you did anything wrong.

This first lawsuit, however, knocked me off of my game. I made decisions out of fear rather than from confidence, believing the decisions were the best I could make at the time. This fear kept me from trying new things, staying on the cutting edge of my practice—things that had differentiated our firm in the marketplace.

While fear hasn't completely left me, I can now recognize when I'm acting out of fear and when I'm letting go and acting with intention.

The results are coming back. I'm feeling youthful again.

No fear! Or at least not so much of it.

Riding on Borrowed Time

I remember an old TV commercial in which the narrator asks if your car is riding on borrowed time, with the intent of causing you to think of how much tread is left on your tires.

Riding on borrowed time is an interesting concept. Have we ever asked ourselves this question about our lives? Is there routine maintenance that we are ignoring? Health, relationships, unfulfilled business, and unfulfilled promises to others and ourselves? Are we riding on borrowed time?

All of us get approximately the same amount of time on this earth. Have you ever noticed how well some people have used their time? How well have you used your time?

If you are not happy with the things you've neglected in your life, it's not too late to change, but it does take desire and perseverence.

My personal coach had me make a list of all of the things that I still wanted to do in my life. Making the list was easy, because there's more to do than life will allow. Upon reviewing the list, he asked me why I wasn't doing any of these things. I had the usual litany of excuses—not ready, too busy, needed to do something else first. He suggested that perhaps I really didn't want to do these things or that I lacked the courage to follow my heart.

I remember writing "do more camping" on my list. My coach taught me a valuable lesson with this item. He said, "Craig, if you really wanted to go camping more, you would." He was right. I wasn't being totally honest with my list, Sure, I wanted to go camping more, but not enough to do something about it.

I went home and really thought hard about my list. I made a new one and prioritized it according to the most important items, the items I could work on immediately and the ones I need help from others to accomplish.

Once I had done this, I at least had a map of the things that I held important enough to work on. Now the hard part. Why did I want these things, and was I willing to work toward obtaining them?

One of the things that was important to me was writing and publishing this book, and I have worked hard to accomplish this goal.

I guess the meaning of this essay is that if you are clear with what you want and why you want it, you have a better chance of obtaining it. It gives focus to your energy and keeps you from living in a "would of, could of, should of" world.

Don't ride on borrowed time!

The Light to Work By

Purpose is the glowing light that guides our life. It is the light we choose to work by. Just like candles that were lit on the desk in olden times, purpose provides the light we need; a warm, soft light that enhances what we are doing.

Living life guided by the light—doing things for the right reasons for us—not caring if it is acceptable by the masses or today's pop culture is purposeful and enriching.

There is great comfort in knowing why you are doing things, and there is peace in knowing that you are doing things purposefully.

Man has searched for the meaning of life since the dawn of time. Our purpose is there, deep inside us, just waiting to be tapped and unleashed. All we need to do is let our guard down and listen to our inner self.

I believe that each of us has a calling, but many of us deny ourselves from it—we tune out while the questions we ask drown out the answers that are living and breathing inside of us.

I have asked these questions for most of my life, hoping that someone would answer them for me—even though I know that only I can answer the questions.

I think that I have found some of the answers, and that is why I began to write. My calling is to teach and share my life experiences. That is my light.

What is yours?

Closing

There are many people that I would like to thank for all of their contributions to this book.

To Sally—thanks for the encouragement, editing, and for finally teaching me about matching subjects with verbs.

To Corin and Carson—thanks for being yourselves.

To Annita and Veronica—thanks for reading, editing and keeping me focused on the finish line.

To Lou—thanks for encouraging me to write, for all of the advice and mentorship, and for the trips to the Wine Country.

To Brian—thanks for the spit and polish.

To those who bought my first book—thanks for the shot in the arm! I hope you enjoy this book, too.

Remember, we all have something to say. All we need is encouragement from friends and family.

Until next time …

Craig

978-0-595-48176-7
0-595-48176-0

www.ingramcontent.com/pod-product-compliance
Lightning Source LLC
Chambersburg PA
CBHW020335290526
45785CB00005B/2033